Just Mini Desserts
Volume 2

More Quick and Easy Mini Desserts

for Casual Entertaining

by Robert Zollweg

Written and Designed by Robert Zollweg
Photography by Rick Luettke, www.luettkestudio.com
Graphics by Gary Raschke and Robert Zollweg
Art Direction Gary Raschke

Library of Congress Cataloging-in-Publication Data:

Just Mini Desserts Volume 2,
More Quick and Easy Mini Desserts
Recipes for Casual Entertaining / Robert Zollweg

ISBN 978-0-615-67330-1

Printed in the United States of America
by R.R. Donnelley and Company

This book is dedicated to

Brenda Bennett

From the very beginning, she supported the concept of developing
cookbooks along with coordinating product.

And to my two very special children,
Christopher and Rhonda

To my mother, Virginia and to my wonderful and understanding family.

A special dedication to Steven and Annie

A very special thanks to Gary Raschke,
with his graphics knowledge and art direction skills,
we made it all happen.

To Bill Muzzillo, my friend at the beach who sometime thinks I'm crazy
but still encourages me to go for it all.

To Karen Barentzen, Beth Baroncini, Cathie Logan, Kelly Kelley,
Denise Grigg, Gina Bacardi, Tom Fratanuono, Serena Williams,
Roger Williams, Jeff Joyce, Joe Mefferd, Greg Pax,
Fran Brietner, Vicki Richardson, Amy Lewarchik,
Brooks Clayton, Sandy Shultz, Melissa Fleig and Emily West.

To Libbey Glass, a great company.

Contents

Introduction   8 - 9

Serving, Containers and Preparation   10 - 17

Puddings and Mousse   18 - 39

Fruit Desserts   40 - 55

Quick and Easy Desserts   56 - 83

Baked Desserts   84 - 97

Not Just For Kids !   98 - 107

Index   108 - 109

Introduction

Just Mini Desserts Two is my second volume cookbook on mini desserts and it is still all about serving delicious desserts in little mini servings. It's as simple as that. But it goes beyond just the desserts. It's about serving these mini desserts in a variety of little containers or dessert dishes and giving your guests a few choices of different desserts. You probably wouldn't bother making mini desserts just for 2 or 3 people, but you would when you are having friends and family over when you need more then one dessert. Making your guests feel welcome and at home. That's what entertaining is all about and Just Mini Desserts Two is here to help. The whole mini dessert trend started at the National Restaurant Show in Chicago a few years ago. Restaurants were seeing a decline in larger, over the top desserts and recognized that many of the guests were watching their weight or being more calorie conscious. As a result, they started developing and serving petite versions or mini-desserts. To make them special and more exciting, they found small glass and ceramic

containers to show off their new creations. They are usually served in multiples with a variety of different mini-desserts to choose from. I felt this was something today's consumers would love to try at home and quite a few retailers have added these wonderful mini dessert sets to their assortment and the results have been fantastic.

Displaying mini desserts is also a key component in entertaining. Presenting them on a variety of different serving and tiered trays helps with this fashionable and trendy presentation. These presentations are great for special parties, wedding showers and birthdays, to name a few. You will look very professional and your guests will love you and

look forward to another one of your parties or get togethers.

I hope you enjoy these new little Mini Desserts Volume Two recipes as much as I have in creating them. They are quick and simple and fun to make.

I love to entertain and mini desserts are a great way to turn a special occasion into something really special.

Enjoy !   Robert Zollweg

Containers, Preparation and Serving Suggestions

When do you serve mini desserts? As I mentioned in my first cookbook on mini desserts, I usually serve mini desserts whenever I'm having a get together, for at least 8 or more people. That way I can make several different recipes and everyone will be happy. For a fabulous dessert table presentation, you can use your kitchen counter, a small card table set up in the living room or family room, dining room table or wherever you decide to serve, the little extra effort with your presentation makes all the difference in the world to your guests.

Containers

There are so many wonderful containers in the marketplace that can be used to serve mini desserts. Use your imagination. Glass makes a wonderful medium because you can see the layering of the ingredients with all the colors and textures.

I have adapted many of my favorite dessert recipes to fit into these mini containers. If you cannot prepare them in small dishes, you can always serve them in small dishes.

13

Preparation

As I mentioned in my first cookbook on mini desserts, there are a number of different tools in the marketplace for making it easier to help fill these small dessert dishes. Pictured above is a commercial decorating press and filling tool, but you can use a simple pastry bag or even a one quart storage bag with the corner cut off. The candy funnel is another great filling tool. Both can be purchased at your area retailers. They are very helpful in filling the smaller items and can also add fancy swirls and a real professional touch. I love to use them. They are simple to operate and very easy to clean.

Supplies

Some simple kitchen tools like a couple of glass mixing bowls in different sizes, a spatula, whisk, some small prep bowls, measuring spoons, a good quality cutting board, some large spoons and a sharp knife, that is about all you really need to prepare most of these simple desserts right in your own home.

15

Serving Presentations

Here, I'm showing a Mini Dessert Tasting Party. It is a little more of an elaborate table setting than you may do every day, but the results are fabulous. Try using a variety of different mini desserts on some square and rectangular platters and servers. They can be made of glass, ceramic or stainless steel. I will also use flavored teas, dessert coffees and mini cocktails to compliment your mini desserts. This can be a wonderful presentation that is ideal for any large get together with family and friends. It may take a little more time, but the results are worth every minute of it and your guests will love it.

Puddings & Mousse

Homemade Chocolate Pudding

There is something about homemade chocolate pudding that is so comforting. Serving it to your guests in little glass dessert dishes at a family get together just makes it all the more special.

You will need 12 of the small dessert dishes, 3-4 oz each, see photo at right.

1 cup sugar
2 tbsp cornstarch
1/4 tsp salt
2 cups whole milk
2 eggs, slightly beaten
2 tbsp butter
1 tsp vanilla
3-4 one ounce squares unsweetened chocolate, chopped
whipped topping for garnish, optional

In a saucepan, blend the sugar, cornstarch, salt, chocolate pieces and milk. Cook over medium heat until thick and bubbly, stirring constantly. Cook two more minutes.

In a mixing bowl, take 2 tbsp of the chocolate mixture from above and mix it with the beaten eggs. Mix well. Return this mixture to the original batch and cook about 2 more minutes. Remove from heat and add the butter and vanilla. Mix well. Pour into the small glass dessert dishes and refrigerate at least an hour. Serve with a dollop of whipped topping and Enjoy !

Tapioca Pudding

There have been all sorts of names from children all over the world for this dessert. British children call it "frog spawn" and American children have been known to call it "fish eyes and glue". It is a traditional old dessert and the consistency of the dessert is a little different but totally delicious.

You will need 12 small glass dessert dishes, 3 oz each, see photo at right.

3 cups whole milk
1/2 cup quick cooking tapioca
1/2 cup white sugar
1/4 tsp salt
2 eggs, beaten
1/2 tsp vanilla

In a medium saucepan, stir together the milk, tapioca, sugar and salt. Bring mixture to boil over medium heat, stirring constantly. Reduce heat to low and cook for another 5 minutes.

In another mixing bowl, mix about a cup of the milk mixture and a tablespoon or so at a time of the beaten eggs until well blended. Return the egg mixture to the original milk mixture and bring to a simmer over low heat for 2 minutes. Stir constantly until it becomes thickened. Remove from heat and stir in the vanilla. Pour into the glass mini dessert dishes. This can sometimes be served warm or you can refrigerate it for an hour or so and serve it cold. Serve and Enjoy !

Rice Pudding

Rice pudding or Arroz Con Leche as the Spanish call it, is a comforting, delicious dessert that has been around for ages. Nothing beats the old fashion cooked version.

You will need 12 glass mini dessert dishes, 3 oz each, see photo at right.

1 cup long grain rice
3 cups water
1 - 3" cinnamon stick
1 tbsp grated lime peel
pinch of salt

2 cups milk
2 cups sugar or 1 cup white sugar and 1 cup brown sugar
1/3 cup raisins
1 tsp vanilla
1 tbsp butter or margarine
ground cinnamon for garnish, optional

Place the rice in a large saucepan with the water, cinnamon stick, grated lime and salt. Bring to boil, lower heat and cook covered until almost all the water has been absorbed.

Stir in the milk, vanilla, butter, raisins and sugar to the rice mixture and cook, stirring constantly over low heat until the mixture thickens.

This can also be made without the raisins.

Remove from heat and let stand 20 minutes. Transfer to the small dessert dishes and sprinkle with cinnamon right before serving. Enjoy !

Lemon Delight

Lemon just has a unique and delicious flavor all of its own. In this dessert, it's creamy smooth and so refreshing. It makes a great mini dessert to serve after a heavy meal.

This will make enough to fill 12 small mini dessert dishes, photo at right.

2 cups graham cracker crumbs
3 tbsp honey

2 cups cold milk
2 pkg lemon instant pudding mix
1 container whipped topping, 8 oz
1 tbsp lemon zest or 1 tsp lemon juice

In a mixing bowl, add the cracker crumbs and honey, mix well. I sometimes put it all in a plastic sandwich bag for ease of mixing and clean up. Put 2 heaping tablespoons of cracker crumbs in the bottom of each dish, pat down.

Pour milk in a large mixing bowl. Add the lemon pudding mix. Beat with a whisk for 2 minutes until thick. Divide mixture in half. Pour half the mixture into each of the mini dessert dishes.

Take the remaining mixture and add about half to two-thirds of the whipped topping and the lemon zest or juice. Mix well. Add some of this mixture to each of the dessert dishes.

Refrigerate for 1-2 hours or until set. Top it off with a dollop of the remaining whipped topping. Serve and Enjoy !

Silky Milk Chocolate Mousse

Who doesn't love the rich taste of a smooth and velvety milk chocolate dessert? You can make it with dark, semi-sweet or sweet chocolate, depending on the intensity of your desired chocolate flavor. I usually use semi-sweet chocolate. The mousse is sweet, but not too sweet.

You will need 12 mini dessert glasses (3 oz each), small glass cordials or square shot glasses. See photo at right.

one package (8 oz) cream cheese, softened
one container (8 oz) whipped topping
2 tbsp sugar
1/4 tsp vanilla
4 oz baking chocolate or chocolate chips
12 raspberries for garnish, optional

In a large mixing bowl, beat softened cream cheese, sugar and vanilla until fluffy.

In another smaller microwavable mixing bowl, melt the chocolate until creamy.

Add chocolate mixture to cream cheese mixture, mix thoroughly. Gently fold in whipped topping. If you want it marbleized, don't mix it very well.

Fill each shot glass to the top with the chocolate mousse. I use my Dessert Pro filling tool with the star tip and it creates a wonderful swirl effect with the mousse. You can garnish with a dollop of whipped topping, a few shavings of chocolate, a chocolate wafer or fresh raspberries as pictured on the right. Serve and Enjoy !

Pina Colada Mousse

Think of yourself on a tropical beach or at a table in a cool cabana next to the pool, savoring a delicious little mini dessert that tastes just like a pina colada. Imagine that !

You will need 12 mini dessert glasses (3 oz each). See photo at right.

one package (8 oz) cream cheese, softened
one container (8 oz) whipped topping
1/4 tsp vanilla
2 tbsp sugar
1/4 cup lime juice
1/4 cup shredded coconut
1/4 cup of coconut milk

In a large mixing bowl, beat softened cream cheese, sugar, lime juice and vanilla until fluffy. Now add the coconut and coconut milk. Blend thoroughly. Fold in the whipped topping.

Fill each mini dessert dish with the mousse. I use my Dessert Pro filling tool with the star tip, which creates a wonderful swirl effect with the mousse. You can garnish with a dollop of whipped topping or a lime wedge. Serve and Enjoy !

Pistachio Pudding

Whenever I make this dessert for a get together, it is one of the first to go (well really the second, anything chocolate always goes first). But it tastes great and makes a beautiful presentation.

You will need 12 mini dessert dishes for a fabulous presentation. See photo at right.

1-1/2 cups graham cracker crumbs
1/4 cup chopped pistachios
1/4 cup honey or half stick butter and 1/4 cup sugar

1 pkg instant pistachio pudding
1 pkg instant vanilla pudding
3 cups cold milk
1 container whipped topping, 8 oz
one drop of green food coloring

In a large mixing bowl, add the 3 cups cold milk, drop of green food coloring and the 2 packages of pudding mix. Mix for 2 minutes until it starts to thicken. Fold in about 1 cup of the whipped topping into a little more than half the pudding mixture. Mix well. Fill each of the mini dessert dishes to about half full. Set aside and let the mixture set-up for a few minutes.

Mix the cracker crumbs and pistachios with the honey until crumbly. Sprinkle about a heaping tablespoon of cracker crumbs on top of the pudding mixture. Smooth out.

Take the remaining pudding mixture and add the rest of the whipped topping and mix well. Fill each dish until almost full. Garnish with a dollop of whipped topping, optional. Refrigerate for an hour or so. Serve and Enjoy !

Cherry Angel Delight

This is a very light and delicious summertime dessert. It's one of my favorites when I need to take a dessert to a family potluck and I don't have all day to prepare something.

You will need 12 small glass dessert dishes, see photo at right.

1 angel food cake
1 large can cherry pie filling
1 large package vanilla instant pudding mix
1-1/2 cups of milk
1 cup of sour cream

Take a slice of angel food cake and cut it into small pieces and fill the bottom of the mini dessert dish. Repeat until all dessert dishes are filled.

In a large glass mixing bowl, combine the pudding mix, milk and sour cream. Stir until mixed thoroughly and it just starts to thicken. Pour immediately over the angel food cake pieces until almost covered. Refrigerate about an hour.

Once set, place a few spoonfuls of cherry pie filing on top of each until covered. Refrigerate until ready to serve. Put the desserts dishes on a long rectangular platter or round glass platter for a wonderful presentation, Serve and Enjoy !

Fruit Desserts

Marshmallow Fruit & Cream

This mini dessert is ideal during the summer months because the fresh melons are so flavorful and sweet. It's perfect for a summer brunch or really anytime.

You will need 12 small mini bowls for serving. See photo at right.

2 cups of marshmallow cream
3 - 4 cups of fresh cantaloupe, honey dew or watermelon, cut into small cubes
a few tablespoons of honey
a few sprigs of fresh mint, optional

In a large mixing bowl, toss the melon cubes with the honey until well coated, being careful not to mush up the melon cubes.

Fill the bottom of each mini bowl with cubed melon. Add a large dollop of marshmallow cream. Fill the rest of the bowl with cubed melon. Garnish with a small dollop of marshmallow cream on top and a few sprigs of fresh mint. Serve and Enjoy !

Coconut Creams

Coconut Creams have just enough coconut to make you think you are somewhere exotic but not enough to make you want to stay out all night and party. This can be made with or without the coconut rum. The coconut rum just adds a little zip and we all need a little zip now and then.

You will need 12 small mini dessert dishes, see photo at right.

1 cup graham cracker crumbs, 1/4 cup finely chopped pecans, 1/4 cup honey

1 large box (5.9 oz) vanilla, banana cream or cheesecake instant pudding
2 cups cold milk
2 cups sour cream
2 cups coconut flakes, divided in half
1/4 cup coconut rum
some whipped topping for garnish, optional

Take about a cup of coconut flakes and place on a cookie sheet and broil in the oven for a few minutes, until golden brown. Watch carefully, as they will darken rather quickly. Set aside.

In a mixing bowl, combine the cracker crumbs, finely chopped pecans and honey and mix well, until crumbly. Fill the bottom of each dish with about 2 heaping tablespoons. Flatten down.

In another large mixing bowl, combine the milk and sour cream. Mix in the pudding mix. Beat as directed on package until it just starts to thicken. Stir in the coconut flakes and coconut rum, blend well. Pour into each dessert dish until almost full. Place in refrigerator until set, usually about an hour or so. Garnish with a dollop of whipped topping and sprinkle with toasted coconut flakes when ready to serve. Enjoy !

Strawberries and Hot Fudge

What makes this little dessert so special is the little ceramic amuse busch dishes. They are just so darn cute and perfect for serving little tasting desserts. Amuse busch is a small delicacy, prepared by the chef to let you experience what is coming for dinner. But in this case, it's a little something after dinner.

You will need 12 of these amuse busch dishes, see photo at right.

1/2 cup hot fudge sauce
12 fresh strawberries
12 chunks of fresh pineapple, optional

Place a tablespoon of hot fudge in the bottom of each amuse busch, not quite half full. Add a fresh strawberry and a small wedge of pineapple next to the strawberry. Place on a tray and you are ready to go. Serve and Enjoy !

Berries & Cream

Follow the recipe on page 28, the pineapple mousse, but substitute the pineapple puree with raspberry puree. Using a cookie press or Dessert Pro, fill each amuse busch with the cream mousse and garnish with fresh raspberries, strawberries and blueberries. Serve and Enjoy !

Orange Delight

I have always made this dessert with orange gelatin. But many of my friends have tried strawberry or raspberry and have loved it. So you decide. This recipe uses orange gelatin, but you can substitute another flavor if you like.

You will need 12 mini dessert dishes, see photo at right.

1 small pkg orange gelatin
2 cups mandarin oranges
1 pkg cream cheese, 4 oz. softened
1 cup mini marshmallows or marshmallow cream
3 tbsp flour
3/4 cup sugar
3/4 cup orange juice
1 cup whipped topping for garnish, optional

Make the orange gelatin as directed. Set aside until it just starts to jell, but don't let it set. Add the mandarin oranges to each dessert dish. Fill each of your mini dessert dishes about half full of gelatin mixture. Place in refrigerator until set.

Cover each of the dessert dishes with a layer of mini marshmallows or marshmallow cream on top of the orange gelatin. return to refrigerator.

In a saucepan, boil flour, sugar and orange juice, stirring constantly. Add the softened cream cheese and mix well. Pour this hot mixture over the marshmallows or marshmallow cream. They will melt slightly. Refrigerate an hour or so. Top with a dollop of whipped topping or orange slice. Serve and Enjoy !

Mini English Trifle

Adapting trifle dessert to a mini dessert dish was kind of a challenge, but I think in the end it worked well and is quite a delicious little mini dessert. You can use almost any fresh fruit. It's really up to you. I like the combination of strawberries, bananas and blueberries, especially when they are in season. They look delicious !

You will need 12 mini bowls, see photo at right.

1 large package vanilla or banana instant pudding
8 oz sour cream
3 bananas, sliced
1 cup blueberries
1 cup fresh strawberries, sliced
3 cups of cold milk
36 vanilla wafers or any small shortbread cookie
about a cup of whipped topping for garnish

Put about 3 of the vanilla wafers in the bottom of each dessert bowl. Set aside.

In a mixing bowl, add the cold milk and instant pudding, mix about 2 minutes until slightly thickened. Add the sour cream and mix well. Pour a good tablespoon of pudding over the wafers. Add a layer of sliced strawberries, bananas and blueberries. Pour another large spoonful of cream mixture over the fresh fruit. Garnish with a dollop of whipped topping or a few extra pieces of fruit. Serve and Enjoy !

Berry Berry Cream Dessert

A dear friend gave me this recipe and has always served it frozen. I like it a little more at room temperature, because it seems creamier. You will have to decide. Either way it is delicious. I like serving it in a mini wine glass or cordial, making it special.

You will need 12 mini wine glasses, see photo at right.

1 can sweetened condensed milk
1/2 cup sour cream
1/2 cup lemon juice
1-1/2 - 2 cups fresh berries (strawberries, raspberries and blackberries)
1 container whipped topping, 8 oz

In a mixing bowl, stir together the sweetened condensed milk, sour cream and the lemon juice. Mix in the fresh berries, saving a few for garnish. Fold in the whipped topping and carefully spoon the mixture into the mini wine glasses. Garnish with a couple of pieces of fresh fruit. Serve and Enjoy !

Caramel Apple Dessert

This dessert is like eating a caramel apple with a spoon. Very rich and delicious. It reminds me when I use to go to a neighborhood carnival as a child, with cotton candy and riding the Tilt-a-Whirl ! But it was the caramel apples that always caught my eye. So I think you'll be pleasantly surprised at this wonderful dessert.

You will need 12 mini dessert dishes, see photo at right.

8 oz cream cheese
1/2 cup brown sugar
1 tsp vanilla
1 container whipped topping, 8 oz
1 cup chopped pecans
3 cups apples, finely chopped, about a 1/2" square
a pinch of cinnamon
1/4 cup caramel topping

In a mixing bowl, beat the cream cheese, brown sugar and vanilla until smooth. Fold in the whipped topping. Add the apples, the pecan pieces and a pinch of cinnamon. Spoon into mini dessert dishes. Drizzle with caramel topping. Serve and Enjoy !

Quick & Easy Desserts

Mint Julip Dessert

This has been said to have originated in Louisville, Kentucky, but we believe Marty from Grand Rapids was sitting on the beach and came up with this wonderful dessert all on his own. It's very simple to make and really has the taste of the derby. We dedicate this dessert recipe to the famous derby horse, I'll Have Another. May he enjoy life in the pasture.

You will need 12 mini square dessert bowls, see photo at right.

Some ready made chocolate brownies, cut into 1' squares
1/4 cup Kentucky Bourbon, the original stuff from Bourbon County, Kentucky
4 oz cream cheese, softened
4 oz whipped topping
1 tbsp sugar
1 tsp vanilla
a drop of green food coloring
a few drops of mint extract
some fresh mint sprigs for garnish

Cut the chocolate brownies into 1" squares and place one in the bottom of each square dessert dish. Poke a hole in the center of each brownie with the handle of a wooden spoon. Drizzle about a teaspoon of bourbon over each brownie.

In a mixing bowl, combine the cream cheese, sugar, vanilla, mint extract and food coloring. Fold in the whipped topping. Add a little milk if needed. This mixture needs to be a little runny. Place a large spoonful of cream cheese mixture on top of each brownie and let it run over the sides. Add more or less depending on what you like. Garnish with a sprig of mint or a small mint cookie. Serve and Enjoy !

Buckeye Bash
aka Go Buckeyes!

I'm not even a Buckeye fan but this dessert tastes just like the candy those folks from Ohio call buckeyes. To me, it tastes like a peanut butter cup. But you decide. If you like peanut butter and chocolate, this one is for you.

You will need 12 mini dessert dishes, see photo at right.

1-1/2 cups graham cracker crumbs
1/4 cup honey

8 oz cream cheese, softened
2 cups powdered sugar
1-1/2 cups peanut butter
4 tbsp half and half or whole milk
16 oz whipped topping, divided
one large box chocolate instant pudding
3 cups cold milk

In a mixing bowl, combine the cracker crumbs and honey until well blended. Add a heaping spoonful to the bottom of each dessert dish.

In another mixing bowl, add the cream cheese, powdered sugar, half and half and peanut butter, mix well. Fold in about 3/4 of the whipped topping. Fill each dessert dish about half full with cream cheese mixture. Set aside.

In a mixing bowl, add the cold milk and instant chocolate pudding. Mix about 2 minutes, just until it starts to thicken. Pour immediately into the dessert dishes until the pudding covers the cream cheese mixture. Garnish with a large dollop of whipped topping. Serve and Enjoy !

Vanilla Cheesecake
(no bake)

This is one of those simple yet very creamy cheesecake recipes that is just too good to be a no bake recipe. It is velvety smooth and very delicious. I like it just plain, but fresh fruit on top is always quite good too.

You will need 12 small 3 oz mini desserts dishes, see photo at right.

1-1/2 cups graham cracker crumbs
1/4 cup margarine, melted
1/4 cup sugar

12 oz cream cheese (softened) or use ricotta cheese
3/4 cup sour cream
1 cup powdered sugar
2 tsp vanilla extract

Mix the cracker crumbs, butter and sugar together and divide the mixture equally between the 12 dessert dishes and press down. Set aside.

Beat the cream cheese, sour cream, powdered sugar and vanilla in large mixing bowl with electric mixer until well blended and fluffy. Pour equally into the 12 dessert dishes, almost to the top. If you are adding fresh fruit, leave a little more room at the top.

Refrigerate until chilled. When ready to serve, top each dessert dish with a spoonful of pie filling or fresh berries or leave plain like I have pictured to the right. I recommend removing this from the refrigerator about 15-20 minutes before serving. Serve and Enjoy !

Lemon Cheesecake
(no bake)

Lemon flavored desserts are becoming one of my favorite flavors of the season. They are light, refreshing, smooth and delicious. The graham cracker crust is optional.

You will need 12 mini dessert dishes, see photo at right.

1 cup graham cracker crumbs
1/4 cup butter or margarine, melted
1 tbsp sugar

1 pkg lemon flavored gelatin (3 oz)
1 cup boiling water
8 oz cream cheese
1 cup white sugar
1 tsp vanilla
1 can evaporated milk (5 oz can)
1 cup whipped topping for garnish, optional

In a mixing bowl, combine cracker crumbs, melted butter and sugar. Mix until well blended. Put a spoonful into the bottom of each dessert dish, pat down.

In a microwaveable bowl, add 1 cup boiling water and lemon gelatin. Mix well. Let cool, but not set. It should be jelled.

In a large bowl, beat cream cheese, white sugar and vanilla until smooth, set aside.

In another mixing bowl, whip evaporated milk until thick and peaks form with an electric mixer. Pour in lemon gelatin and mix well. Fold in cream cheese mixture. Mix until smooth. Fill the dessert dishes and refrigerate for at least an hour or so. When ready to serve, add a dollop of whipped topping and Enjoy !

Mango Chiffon Dessert

If you like the taste of orange or mango and who doesn't, you will love this dessert. Velvety smooth and not real sweet. I really like both versions. They are equally delicious. You will need 12 mini-dessert dishes, about 4-5 oz each. I choose the little brandy glasses, they are small and so cute. They serve just enough of this tangy dessert to compliment your other specialties. See photo at right.

6 egg yolks, slightly beaten
2 cups water
2 pkg (3 oz) mango gelatin
6 tsp grated fresh mango

16 oz whipped topping
1/2 cup sugar
1/2 cup mango-orange juice
1 cup water

Combine egg yolks and two cups water in saucepan, add 1/2 cup sugar. Cook and stir over low heat until mixture slightly thickens and just comes to a boil. Remove from heat. Add gelatin and stir until dissolved. Add 1 cup water, mango-orange juice and fresh mango to the egg mixture. Stir thoroughly and refrigerate until slightly thickened or jelled.

Add the whipped topping to the jelled mixture. Blend well, use an electric mixer for a real creamy texture. Spoon into dessert dishes and chill until firm, about 2-3 hours. Garnish with a piece of fresh mango or a dollop of whipped topping. Serve and Enjoy !

Orange Chiffon Dessert

Substitute orange juice for the mango juice and orange zest for the fresh mango and follow the basic directions from above. This will taste just like a creamcicle. Delicious !

Banana Caramel Cream Dessert

This dessert is pretty simple but is bursting with flavor. The combination of bananas, caramel and pecans is incredible. If you are serving this dessert immediately, you could substitute the cream cheese mixture with vanilla ice cream. Now it is a praline sundae.

You will need 12 small glass dessert bowls, 4 oz each. See photo at right.

4-6 ripe bananas (firm) sliced
8 oz cream cheese, softened
4 tbsp whipped topping
1/2 cup sugar
1/2 cup caramel sauce
1/2 cup chopped pecans or peanuts

Mix together in a mixing bowl the softened cream cheese, whipped topping and sugar. Add a spoonful of this mixture in the bottom of each mini dessert dish. Place 5-6 slices of bananas in each dish on top of the cream cheese mixture; drizzle with caramel sauce and sprinkle with nut pieces. It's that simple. Serve and Enjoy !

And if you really want to go over the top, add a dollop of hot fudge. Serve and Enjoy !

Chocolate Raspberry Creams

Many of my friends just crave anything made with chocolate and raspberries. This one is very easy and the results are delicious. Perfect for a large get together when you need a lot of different mini desserts.

You will need 12 shot glasses or mini dessert dishes, see photo at right.

1 package (8 oz) cream cheese, softened and divided
1 container whipped topping (16 oz) divided
1/4 cup sugar, divided
2 tsp vanilla, divided
2 oz Baker's Chocolate
1/2 cup fresh or frozen raspberries, mashed
one drop of red food coloring, optional
12 whole fresh raspberries for garnish

Divide the cream cheese in half. In a mixing bowl, place half the cream creese, half the sugar and 1 tsp vanilla. Mix well. In another small microwaveable bowl, melt the chocolate until creamy (be careful not to let it burn). I always microwave it for a few seconds at a time, stirring every time. Combine the chocolate into the cream cheese mixture. Mix well. Add half the whipped topping and mix again. Fill each dessert dish or shot glass half full of the chocolate mixture and tap down. Set aside.

In another mixing bowl, add the remaining softened cream cheese, vanilla and sugar. Mix well. Fold in the crushed raspberries, red food coloring and mix again. Here is where I use the Dessert Pro to fill the raspberry cream on top of the chocolate cream. You can spoon it on top but the Dessert Pro will make them very pretty and delicious. Garnish with a fresh raspberry and refrigerate an hour or so. Remove from refrigerator half hour before serving so they will be creamy. Enjoy !

Dizzy Izzy Delightful Fluff

This is another recipe from a family member who has been making it for years for all our holiday get togethers. Joyce Izzi is not dizzy at all but I thought the name sounded kind of fun. She has always called it Pink Junk. It is very light and creamy and pretty easy to make. You can use strawberries or raspberries. Both versions are delicious.

You will need 12 mini dessert dishes, see photo at right.

2 - 3 oz packages of strawberry gelatin
2 - 10 oz packages of frozen strawberries, thawed
1 large container whipped topping
3 cups water
6 strawberries cut in half for garnish, optional

Boil 2 cups of water in a microwaveable bowl. Add the strawberry gelatin and mix until completely dissolved. Add one cup cold water and thawed strawberries with the juice. mix well and let soft-set or until gelled.

Mix the whipped topping with the gelatin mixture and pour into the mini dessert dishes. If you have some left over, pour into another small bowl. Garnish the mini dishes with a strawberry half or a few chopped pieces and a dollop of whipped topping. Refrigerate for an hour or so. Serve and Enjoy !

Brownie Sundae

This is just a cute little ice cream sundae that will please almost everyone. The only one who won't like it is someone who would want a great big dish of it. But this little sundae is perfect for after dinner or for a little treat, just when you need it.

You will need 12 mini dessert dishes, see photo at right.

12 small 1" square or round chocolate brownies
about a quart of vanilla or chocolate ice cream
Some hot fudge sauce
1/2 cup of toffee pieces
1/2 cup of chopped pecans

Place the brownies in the bottom of the mini dessert dish. Add a generous scoop of ice cream on top of the brownie. Add a spoonful of hot fudge sauce and then sprinkle with toffee and pecan pieces. Serve immediately and Enjoy !

Classic Ambrosia

This dessert has been around for years and is called many different names depending on the ingredients. It is known as the "food of the gods" in Greek and Roman mythology, so I guess it's somewhat fitting.

You will need 12 mini dessert dishes, see photo at right.

1 cup whipped topping
6 oz sour cream
1 tbsp white sugar
1 cup mini marshmallows
1 cup mandarin oranges, well drained
1 cup fresh pineapple (canned chunks will work)
1 cup shredded coconut
1/2 cup chopped pecans
1/2 cup maraschino cherries, sliced in half

For variations, you can add sliced bananas, sliced peaches or pears

In a large mixing bowl, add the whipped topping, sour cream and sugar. Mix well. Fold in the remaining ingredients. Refrigerate. When ready to serve, fill your mini dessert dishes and garnish with an additional maraschino cherry on top. Serve and Enjoy !

Raspberry Fudge Dessert

This is another one of those delicious chocolate and raspberry desserts that is very chocolatey and rich, but smooth as silk. It can be made with or without the graham cracker crust on the bottom. I like the cracker crust, because it adds a little surprise at the bottom.

This recipe makes 12 servings in small glass dessert dishes or glass shooters, 2-3 oz each. See photo at right.

6 - 7 whole chocolate graham crackers, crushed
2-3 tbsp honey

2 cups (16 oz) whipping cream
12 oz semi-sweet chocolate chips
1/2 cup pecans, finely chopped, optional
2 tbsp unsweetened cocoa powder
2 oz cream cheese
1/4 cup sugar
1 cup fresh raspberries, pureed or 1/2 cup raspberry jam

Crush graham crackers and mix with 3 tbsp honey. Divide equally in the bottom of the 12 small dishes, pat down. Add a spoonful of raspberry puree or jam.

In a heavy saucepan, bring the whipping cream just to a boil, reduce heat to low and simmer 5 minutes, stirring constantly. Add chocolate chips, cream cheese, sugar and cocoa powder and mix until smooth and melted. Stir in pecan pieces (optional). Pour chocolate mixture into each dish over raspberry and crust. Chill 1 hour or so.

Remove from refrigerator about 30 minutes before serving. Finish off with another spoonful of raspberry puree on top when you are ready to serve. Enjoy !

Chocolate Mocha Dessert

Ask any coffee lover, the combination of chocolate and coffee is pure heaven. This creamy dessert is perfect with a cup of strong java while watching a beautiful sunset and gossiping with a close friend, or both.

You will need 12 mini dessert dishes, see photo at right.

1 cup granola, finely crushed
8 oz cream cheese
1 cup powdered sugar
8 oz whipped topping, divided
1 tbsp chocolate syrup
1/4 tsp vanilla
2 small pkg of instant chocolate pudding
3 cups of whole milk
1/4 cup strong black coffee

cherries, nuts or chocolate shavings for garnish, all optional

Place a spoonful of granola in the bottom of each dessert dish. In a mixing bowl, add the cream cheese, 6 oz of the whipped topping, chocolate syrup, vanilla, powdered sugar and black coffee. Mix until smooth and creamy. Fill each dessert dish about half full of this mixture. Set aside.

In another mixing bowl, add the milk and chocolate pudding, beat about 2 minutes until it just starts to thicken. Pour immediately on top of the cream cheese mixture in the dessert dishes. Refrigerate about an hour. When ready to serve, add a dollop of whipped topping and a few chocolate shavings. Serve and Enjoy !

Sweet & Salty Chocolate Pizzazz

Most of my friends all agreed, the combination of something sweet and salty was a must in my new dessert book. This was a collaboration among all of us. Hope you enjoy it.

You will need 12 mini dessert dishes, see photo at right.

2 cups mini pretzels, the smaller the better, crushed
1/2 cup salted peanuts or pecans, finely chopped
1/4 cup butter or honey
6 oz chocolate chips
1 cup whipping cream
1 tbsp cocoa
2 oz cream cheese
3 tbsp sugar
1/4 cup chopped pecans or peanuts for garnish
some caramel ice cream topping for garnish

Mix the crushed pretzels and peanuts together with the butter or honey. They need to be well coated. Fill the bottom of the mini dessert dish about half to 3/4 full with this pretzel mixture.

In a saucepan, add the whipping cream and bring almost to a boil and then cook for an additional 4-5 minutes on low heat. Remove from heat and add the cocoa, cream cheese, sugar and chocolate chips. Stir until completely smooth. Pour the hot chocolate mixture over the pretzels and pecan pieces until almost covered. Let cool for 30 minutes. Sprinkle with remaining pecan pieces and a spoonful of caramel sauce. Serve and Enjoy !

Baked Desserts

Sweet Potato Pie

This recipe has been in my family for years. It can work as a side dish as well as a delicious dessert. I make it a little less sweet for a side dish.

You will need 12 mini baking dishes, see photo at right.

Set oven to 350 degrees

one large can yams or sweet potatoes
2 cups dark brown sugar, divided
1/2 cup butter, melted, divided
1/4 tsp vanilla
1/2 cup whipping cream or half and half
1 cup pecans, finely chopped

In a large, microwaveable mixing bowl, place the sweet potatoes and microwave for about 3-4 minutes until warm. Mash these until chunky. Stir in 1 cup dark brown sugar, 1/4 cup butter, vanilla and whipping cream. With an electric mixer, mix until smooth and creamy. Fill your mini baking crocks about 3/4 full. Set aside.

In another mixing bowl, place the other cup of dark brown sugar and melted butter. Mix until creamy. Mix in the pecan pieces and blend well. Place a heaping spoonful or so on top of each of the dishes until covered.

Place crocks on a cookie sheet and bake in the oven at 350 degrees for about 30 minutes or until heated through. Serve and Enjoy !

Fruit Tarts

This is one of my favorite mini desserts for the fall season. Little fruit tarts will please everyone. They can be made with almost any fresh or canned fruit.

You will need 12 small ceramic crocks or ramekins, 3-4 oz each. Make sure they are suitable for baking. See photo at right. Preheat oven to 350 degrees.

Use any kind of fresh fruit (strawberries, raspberries, blueberries, apples or peaches). You can also use canned fruit or pie filling.

3 cups of cleaned sliced fruit (do not slice the raspberries or blueberries)

1/4 cup flour	1/2 cup flour
1/2 cup sugar	1/4 cup sugar
1/4 tsp almond extract	1/4 cup brown sugar
pinch of cinnamon for the apples or peach tarts	3 tbsp butter or margarine

In a large mixing bowl, combine 1/4 cup flour, sugar and cinnamon (if needed). Add sliced fruit and almond extract, toss gently until well coated. Place enough fruit into the ramekin to fill almost full.

If you use canned pie filling, omit the flour, sugar and almond extract that is mixed with the fruit. I still add a little cinnamon even to canned pie filling.

Crumb Topping
In another mixing bowl, combine 1/2 cup flour and both sugars. Cut in or crumble butter with a pastry blender or a fork until it is crumbly. Cover the top of each baking dish with crumb mixture. Bake in the oven at 350 degrees until just bubbly, about 20-30 minutes. Do not overbake, crunchy fruit is better than soggy fruit. Sometimes I just sprinkle the top with plain granola instead of making the crumb topping. You will need about 2 cups of granola to cover 12 mini crocks. Let cool. Serve and Enjoy !

Baked Pecan Mini Tarts

This is a little more like a traditional pecan pie but smaller and a little more crunchy. It can be made with or without the granola topping, but the topping adds the crunch and makes it a little different from your normal pecan pie.

You will need 12 small ramekins or mini baking dishes, see photo at right. Preheat oven to 350 degrees.

1 cup graham cracker crumbs
1/4 cup butter or margarine, melted
1 tbsp sugar

2 cups granola, finely crushed

1-1/2 cups pecans, slightly chopped in large pieces
1 cup karo syrup, dark brown
3 eggs, slightly beaten
1 cup sugar
2 tbsp butter or margarine, melted
1 tsp vanilla
some whipped topping for garnish, optional

In a mixing bowl, combine the graham cracker crumbs, sugar and melted butter until crumbly. Add a heaping spoonful of cracker crumbs to the bottom of each mini baking dish. Pat down.

In another mixing bowl, add the karo syrup, eggs, sugar, butter. Mix well. Stir in the pecans until well coated. Pour into each of the small baking dishes. Top each with a heaping spoonful of granola until covered. Bake in preheated oven at 350 degrees for about 40-45 minutes. Let cool. Can be served with a dollop of whipped topping. Serve and Enjoy !

Cinnamon Raisin Bread Pudding

Bread pudding is one of those delicious desserts that is made in a hundred different ways. This recipe is from a good friend who believes it was from her great grandmother's recipe box down in Mississippi (now that's a whole other story). But it is still really delicious.

You will need 12 mini baking dishes, see photo at right.

Set oven for 350 degrees

3 cups cubed day old bread
1 cup dark brown sugar
4 eggs, beaten
2 cups of apples, peeled and diced small
2 cups milk
1/2 stick butter, melted
1/2 cup raisins
1 cup pecans, chopped
2 tsp vanilla
2 tsp cinnamon
1/2 tsp pumpkin spice
1 cup heavy cream or whipped topping for garnish, optional

Microwave the apples for a few minutes until crunchy, do not overcook. In a large mixing bowl, add the eggs, vanilla, pumpkin spice, milk, sugar. Mix well. Add the apples, raisins, pecans and cubed bread. Mix until everything is well blended.

Fill each of the mini baking dishes about 3/4 full of bread mixture. Bake at 350 degrees for about 30 minutes. Mixture will rise above the container and settle down once it cools. Serve warm or at room temperature. Garnish with a dollop of whipped topping or a spoonful of heavy cream. Serve and Enjoy !

Blueberry Creams

When blueberries are in season up on Lake Michigan, there is nothing better than these blueberry creams. They are sweet and actually very good for you. I've used blueberries in this recipe, but you can use raspberries, strawberries, blackberries or currants.

You will need 12 mini baking dishes, see photo at right.

Preheat oven to 350 degrees

2 jars blueberry preserves or jelly (12oz each)
3 cups sour cream
2 tbsp dark brown sugar
2 tsp cinnamon
3 pints fresh blueberries

In a small saucepan, bring preserves to a boil. Lower heat and cook until it thickens.

In a mixing bowl, combine the sour cream, cinnamon and sugar. Set aside.

Fill each baking dish with blueberries, about half full. Pour the melted preserves over the blueberries until covered. Pour the sour cream mixture over the blueberries until covered and almost to the top of the baking dish.

Bake in the oven at 350 degrees for about 10 minutes or until the top is slightly browned. Refrigerate an hour or so before serving, but serve at room temperature. Enjoy !

Strawberry-Rhubarb Crunch

The original recipe calls for using just rhubarb, but I like to add fresh strawberries because it takes away the slightly tart flavor of rhubarb. This combination is very subtle yet quite delicious.

You will need 12 mini baking dishes, see photo at right.

Topping:
1 cup flour
1 cup dark brown sugar
1 cup uncooked oatmeal
1/2 cup melted butter or margarine
1 tsp cinnamon

Filling:
1 cup white sugar
2 tbsp cornstarch
1 cup water
1 tsp vanilla
1 drop red food coloring, optional

3 cups diced rhubarb
3 cups sliced strawberries

Mix the first 5 topping ingredients until crumbly. Use half this mixture and fill the bottoms of each mini baking dish. Then fill each dish with strawberries and rhubarb pieces.

In a saucepan, combine the remaining filling ingredients and cook until thick and clear. Pour this mixture over the strawberries and rhubarb. Use the remaining crumb mixture and cover each of the baking dishes.

Bake at 350 degrees for about 30 minutes. They should be a little bubbly. Serve warm or at room temperature. Enjoy !

Not Just For Kids!

Crazy Gelatin Parfaits

This is a really simple yet creamy and delicious gelatin dessert. What makes it extra special is serving it in a small mini parfait glasses. Using fun flavors will make it all the more appealing to kids, but the big kids will go for it also.

You will need 12 tall parfait shooter glasses, 4 oz each. Something tall and skinny that will show the layers. See photo at right.

1 - 3 oz box blueberry gelatin
1 - 3 oz box grape gelatin
some fresh fruit: blueberries and blackberries for these flavors
1 - 8 oz container of whipped topping
3 cups boiling water
some ice cubes

In a mixing bowl, add 1 cup boiling water to one box of grape gelatin, stir until dissolved, about 2 minutes. Add a 1/2 cup ice cubes, stir until melted. Add your favorite fresh or canned fruit to the bottom of the parfait glass, like blackberries or it is just as festive plain. Pour the grape gelatin into the tall shooter glasses until about half full. Refrigerate while making second box of blue gelatin. This will set while making the second box.2

The second layer can be prepared same as the first or follow the next step.

Prepare the second box of gelatin as directed from above, except this time, instead of adding the ice cubes, add 1 cup of whipped topping, mix thoroughly. Add several blueberries on top of the grape gelatin and then pour the blue gelatin into each of the cordial glasses over the blueberries until full. Refrigerate about 2 hours or until set.

When ready to serve, add a dollop of remaining whipped topping. Serve and Enjoy !

Party Parfaits

These are ideal for a brunch or any party when you want something a little more healthy but special and equally delicious. They can be made with almost any type of fresh or canned fruit, but fresh berries are a perfect match along with the vanilla yogurt.

You will need 12 mini parfait glasses, see photo at right.

2 cups vanilla yogurt
some fresh fruit (blueberries, strawberries or blackberries or pineapple and strawberries)
1/2 cup of granola for topping

Put about a half inch of yogurt in the bottom of each mini parfait glass. Add some fresh fruit and then fill with yogurt. Top off with some crunchy granola. Serve and Enjoy !

Phantom Parfaits

This is a great one for the kids. Combining unusual condiments will add to their surprise and delight. Follow the recipe from above but instead of using fresh fruit use chocolate syrup, chocolates chips and peanuts. They'll love it. Serve and Enjoy !

Fruit Smoothie

This is a very smooth and refreshing dessert that is great at breakfast or brunch. These also make great after school snacks for the kids. They can be made with almost any fruit.

You will need a blender and 12 tall mini parfait glasses, 5-6 oz each. See photo at right.

2 cups vanilla yogurt
6 oz whipped topping
12 oz bag frozen mixed berries, thawed
1 cup crushed ice
12 fresh raspberries or strawberries for garnish (optional)

Slightly chop or puree the mixed berries. Sometimes I put the fruit in a blender, blend for a few seconds and then add the yogurt with a few ice cubes and the whipped topping, puree until smooth. It really does not matter how you blend a smoothie. Put everything in all at once and blend. The results are pretty much the same. Smooth and delicious.

Fill shooter glasses with smoothie mixture and add a fun straw and a berry on top for garnish. Refrigerate or serve immediately.

These are light and fluffy. Kids will love them, adults too.   Serve and Enjoy !

Silly Dilly Desserts

These are crazy little desserts that kids today can relate to. With a name like Silly Dilly, they have to be a little strange. Adding all sorts of funky candies, sprinkles and other toppings just makes it all the more appealing, especially to the younger ones.

You will need 12 mini dessert dishes, see photo at right.

1 cup marshmallow cream
1 large box instant chocolate pudding or any flavor the kids will love
3 cups cold milk

You'll need several different kinds of toppings, like M&M's, Resees Pieces, Gummy Bears or Worms, sprinkles, chocolate chips, chopped peanuts, coconut, etc.

Place a spoonful of marshmallow cream in the bottom of each mini dessert dish. Sprinkle a few condiments on top of the marshmallow cream (M&M's, Gummy Bears, etc.).

In a mixing bowl, add the 3 cups milk and the box of instant chocolate pudding. Mix for about 2 minutes until it starts to thicken. Pour immediately into the dessert dishes to cover the marshmallow cream.

Now for the fun part. Add any toppings you like. The more the better. Kids just love all the goop on top. This can be made ahead of time for a party or served immediately. Enjoy !

INDEX

BAKED DESSERTS   84

    Blueberry Creams   94
    Cinnamon Raisin Bread Pudding   92
    Fruit Tarts   88
    Pecan Tarts   90
    Strawberry Rhubarb Crunch   96
    Sweet Potato Pie   86

CONTAINERS, PREPARATION & SERVINGS   10

FRUIT DESSERTS   40

    Berry Berry Cream   52
    Berries & Cream   46
    Caramel Apple Dessert   54
    Coconut Creams   44
    Marshmallow Fruit & Cream   42
    Mini English Trifles   50
    Orange Delight   48
    Strawberries & Hot Fudge   46

NOT JUST FOR KIDS   98

    Crazy Gelatin Parfaits   100
    Fruit Smoothies   104
    Party Parfaits   102
    Phantom Parfaits   102
    Silly Dilly Desserts   106

QUICK & EASY DESSERTS   56

    Banana Caramel Creams   68
    Buckeye Bash   60
    Brownie Sundae   74
    Chocolate Mocha Desserts   80
    Chocolate Raspberry Creams   70
    Classic Ambrosia   76
    Dizzy Izzy Delightful Fluff   72
    Lemon Cheesecake   64
    Mango Chiffon Dessert   66
    Mint Julip Dessert   58
    Orange Chiffon desert   66
    Raspberry Fudge Dessert   78
    Sweet & Salty Chocolate Pizzazz   82
    Vanilla Cheesecake   62

PUDDINGS & MOUSSE   18

    Cherry Angel Delight   36
    Homemade Chocolate Pudding   20
    Key Lime Mousse   28
    Lemon Delight   26
    Pistachio Pudding   34
    Pina Colada Mousse   32
    Pineapple Mousse   28
    Raspberry Custard   36
    Rice Pudding   24
    Silky Chocolate Mousse   30
    Tapioca Pudding   22

About the author.

ROBERT ZOLLWEG is a native of Toledo, Ohio and has been entertaining professionally for many years. Writing this cookbook on Just Mini Desserts, Volume Two is something everyone has asked for since the introduction of the original Just Desserts cookbook. He has worked in the tabletop industry for almost 40 years. He designs glassware, flatware and ceramic product for the retail and foodservice industry. He has worked with all of the major retailers; Bed Bath & Beyond, Crate and Barrel, Pier One Imports, Williams-Sonoma, Macy's, Cost Plus World Market, JCPenneys, Target, Walmart, Home Outfitters and Sears to name a few. He has worked most of his professional career for Libbey Glass in Toledo.

Robert has traveled the world extensively looking for color and design trends and the right product to design and bring to the retail and foodservice marketplace. His collection of mini desserts, tasting and mini cocktail cookbooks have been international best sellers. He is also an artist-painter in his spare time and works primarily with acrylic on canvass using bold colors that has been called by many as abstract expressionism. He has always had a passion for entertaining, so volume two on mini desserts will continue this passion. He currently lives in his historic home in Toledo's Historic Old West End and in the artist community of Saugatuck, Michigan.

To find out more about Robert, visit his web site at: www.zollwegart.com

I hope you have enjoyed this new cookbook on Just Desserts, Volume Two. All my other cookbooks on mini desserts, tastings, cocktails and baking are available at area retailers or on my web site at: www.zollwegart.com